HEALING - THE SHAMAN'S WAY
BOOK 6 – ANIMAL CHAKRAS

Norman W. Wilson PhD

HEALING - THE SHAMAN'S WAY
BOOK 6 – ANIMAL CHAKRAS

Cover Design by
S.R. Walker Designs
www.srwalkerdesigns.com

Interior Design
Omar Lopez, PhD

FICTION4ALL

A FICTION4ALL PAPERBACK

©Copyright 2024

Norman W. Wilson, PhD
The right of Norman W. Wilson to be identified as author and channel of this work has been asserted by him in accordance with the Copyright , Designs and Patents Act 1988.

All Rights Reserved

No reproduction, copy or transmission of the publication may be made without written permission.

No paragraph of this publication may be reproduced, copied, or transmitted say with the written permission of the publisher, or in accordance with the provisions of the Copyright Act 1956 (as amended).

Any person who does any unauthorized act in relation to his publication may be liable to criminal prosecution and civil claims for damages.

ISBN: 978 1 78695 884 6

Published by Fiction4All.
www.fiction4all.com
This edition published 2024

DISCLAIMER

There are no guarantees that any of the suggestions and or procedures described herein will work. Before following the use of any of these suggestions and or procedures always consult your veterinarian. Persons under the age of eighteen should not attempt these suggestions and or procedures. Please remember you are responsible for how you use the information contained in this book.

Norman W. Wilson,
07/2024

APPRECIATION

I am grateful for the faith, the encouragement, and the help I have received in creating this book. I am especially appreciative of my editor and publisher, Stuart Holland, of my cover designer, Stephen R. Walker Designs, for the interior design, Dr. Omar Lopez and for Suzanne, my wife for her continued support.

CHAPTER ONE

OVERVIEW

While scientific research hasn't provided direct validation of the existence of Chakras, the concept of energy centers has been around since 1500 BCE. That is the earliest date for Chakra as a healing technique mentioned in the *Vedas* of the Hindus. It was and is a part of Ayurvedic Medicine. One of its purposes is to balance the energy centers of one's body or to unblock them. These centers are like spinning vortexes and are located along the base of the spine to the top of one's head.

According to the Ancient Indian Hindu traditions, each chakra is a correspondent of specific physical, mental, and emotional functions. These spinning vortexes sometimes face strong opposing forces, resulting in obstructions or blockages of the natural energy flow. As a result of these blockages, the individual may suffer headaches, abdominal upset, anxiety, malcontent, depression, weight loss or gain, and fatigue.

It is believed that like humans, animals have chakras. These spots of energy vortices, traditionally called Petals, flow along an auric meridian system into the physical body. This energy flows in and out of plants and animals, especially in cats, dogs, horses, and other large animals as it does in human beings. Whatever the stimulus it leaves its mark in the aura and impacts the physical and emotional life of the animal. Different color vibrations are emitted by animal chakras and are nearly the same as in humans. The difference is the alignment of the chakras. In cats and dogs, horses, and cows for example, the chakra positions are horizontal *instead of vertical.*

Like humans, animals have an *Etheric System.* What is the Etheric Body System? Simply put, it is the energy system of the physical body. There are three major parts of the Etheric Field: Nadis, Chakras, Aura:

Nadis does not mean nerve. The word Nadis is from the Sanskrit and means channel or pathway. It references a network from which energy flows in human and animal bodies. Literature refers to 72,000 Nadis in the human body and these are divided into three principal Nadis. *Ida* means comfort and is to left of the spine, *Pingala* is to the right of the spine and mirrors Ida. *Sushumna* runs along the spine from the base to the head.

Admittedly, the whole concept of Nadis in animals is not really presented in the ancient texts. However, because many traditional Hindu practices hold that animals possess energy and have energetic structures, it has come into modern practice, that like human beings, other animal forms have Nadis through which energy flows.

Chakra in various spiritual traditions, is considered to be an energy center within the subtle body, which is believed to exist alongside the physical body. The term "chakra" comes from Sanskrit and translates to "wheel" or "disk," indicating the spinning nature of these energy centers. Sometimes vortex is used as the descriptive word for physical nature of these energy systems. The function of chakras is multifaceted and is often described in terms of their influence on physical, emotional, psychological, and spiritual well-being. Here are some key aspects of the function of chakras:

Energy Regulation: Chakras are believed to be responsible for the intake, transformation, and distribution of subtle energy (prana or chi) throughout the body. This energy is thought to be vital for physical health and vitality, as well as for maintaining emotional and mental balance.

Integration of Mind, Body, and Spirit: Each chakra is associated with specific aspects of human experience, including physical organs, emotions, psychological functions, and spiritual qualities. The balanced functioning of chakras is said to contribute to overall harmony and integration of these different aspects of self.

Psychological and Emotional Balance: Imbalances or blockages in chakras are believed to manifest as physical, emotional, or psychological symptoms. For example, an imbalance in the heart chakra may lead to issues with love and compassion, while an imbalance in the throat chakra may affect communication and self-expression.

Spiritual Growth and Awakening: Chakras are often seen as pathways to higher states of consciousness and spiritual realization.

Connection to Universal Consciousness: The highest chakra, the Crown chakra, is associated with universal consciousness.

Aura is different than Chakra in that it is area around the body that radiates energy out, rather than channeling it inside. While the chakra energy is present in the body, the aura is the energy that surrounds it. The auras are filled with seven layers, emitting various colors to reflect your personality, mood, and overall state of health.
Here is an illustration showing the AURA color locations around the body of the seven chakras, and then a list of those colors and their meanings.

Red aura suggests a high levels of vigor, passion, ambition, drive, and leadership are linked to red auras. Individuals with primarily red auras are often gregarious, vivacious, and energetic. They are born leaders, unafraid to assume responsibility and relentlessly pursue their objectives.

Orange aura represents an optimistic, creative, and life-loving attitude. People that have a strong orange aura are typically outgoing, charming, and full of energy.

Yellow aura represents analytical prowess, intellectual vigor, and curiosity. People that have yellow auras most of the time are intelligent and eager to learn new things.

Green aura represents an affinity for nature, nurturing, and healing. People that have a strong green aura are typically very steady and grounded.

Blue aura represents objectivity, intelligence, and spiritual force. Those with a predominately blue aura are calm and have a rich inner life because they have a strong spiritual bond.

Indigo aura's deep shade is symbolic of wisdom, intuition, and a strong bond with the subconscious.

Purple auras in general are also thought to appear in visionaries with significant leadership potential, however they are less transient than indigo auras.

There is some dispute as to how far an aura extends beyond the body. Some authorities claim its one inch from the body; others claim the aura extends about 2 feet from the body while others claim the aura extends on into infinity

CHAPTER TWO

ANIMAL CHAKRAS

Most animals have 8 major chakras, up to 21 minor chakras and 6 smaller energy points called *Bud Chakras*. These *Budd Chakras* are the animals' 4 paw pads, and a patch of skin at the opening of each ear. There is a chakra unique to animals; an extra one in addition to the 8. It the *Brachial or Key Chakra*, identified by famous animal healer, Margrit Coates.

The Brachial Chakra is located on either side of the animal's body in the shoulder areas. This chakra is important because it is the main energy center in animals and as a consequence, it is the area that relates to the animal's interaction with humans. Healing your pet or animal should always begin with the Brachial.

The six Budd Chakras are sensitive to subtle energy vibrations that humans do not generally pick up. They tune into forthcoming changes in the weather. The feet Budd Chakras sense energy vibrations in the earth which are beneficial to the health of the animal.

The 21 minor chakras are located the animal's energy centers and are distributed all over the body: Nose, tail, legs, tongue, and ears. Animal chakras can be stimulated for training and or healing purposes. The location of the animal chakras is shown the following charts. The first chart also shows the color associated with the chakra. The second shows the color and location of the chakras on a horse and the third, shows the chakra location and colors in a dog and cat. Take a few minutes to read the charts.

ANIMAL CHAKRAS' LOCATIONS

CHAKRA	COLOR	LOCATION
Root	Red	Base of tail
Sacral	Orange	Lower Belly
Solar Plexus	Yellow	Upper Chest
Heart	Green	Heart
Throat	Blue	Throat
Sacral	Black	Shoulders
Brow	Indigo	Between the eyes
Crown	Violet	Top of Head
Brachial	Black	Front of leg

CHAKRA LOCATIONS IN A HORSE

Note the location of the chakras. They are horizontal. The same holds true for cows and sheep.

DOG AND CAT CHAKRAS' LOCATIONS

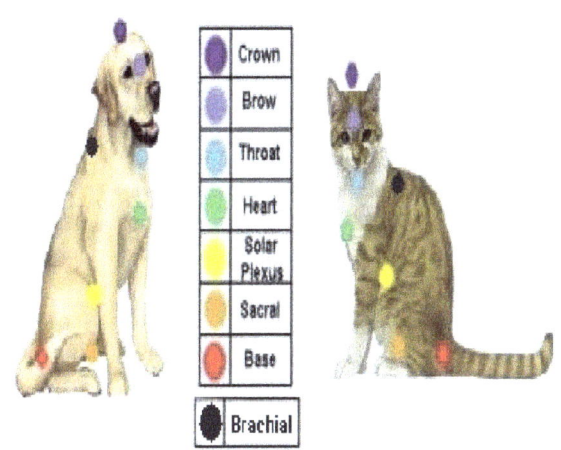

Animal Chakra Points

Animals as well as humans show signs when the chakras are out of balance. It takes a bit of practice to identify the signals that indicate an imbalance and potential health issues in your pet. The following chart shows some of the potential symptoms a cat or dog may show when it is experiencing an imbalance in one or more of their chakras. This is a limited list.

SYMPTOMS OF CHAKRA IMBALANCE

CHAKRA	SYMPTOM
Root	Fearful, Restless Sacral, Whinny meowing
Solar Plexus	Aggressive
Heart	Dejected, jealous,
Throat	Noisy, disobedient
Brow	Distant, distracted
Crown	Depression
Brachial	No touching

ACTIVITY 1

The Tender Touch

Before attempting to check your pet's chakras there is some necessary preparation. Bring yourself into a healing state of mind. You can do this by the following: Meditate for 15 minutes before examining your pet. Softly hum the OM sound, or do a 5- to 10-minute-deep breathing exercise

Wash your hands and dry them. Consider using Lavender Hydrosol. Then, massage your hands to bring about a full blood flow.

What You Will Need:

An EMF Reader. These are available on the Internet. Prices vary based on the brand and sophistication. It is not necessary to purchase an EMF reader. In book five of this series, EMF is discussed and a technique for making a reader or Dowsing Rod as they are also called. In *Healing-The Shaman's Way: Using Vibration to Heal (Zadkiel Publishing 2024 pp. 60-67)* I have written a detailed discussion of EMF and how to make an EMF Reader of Dowsing Rod. Because the Healing-The Shaman's Way books are not inter-dependent, I include the steps for creating an EMF and how to use it with your pet.

You will need the following items:

A mental clothes hanger, a pair of wire cutters, and one plastic straw.

Directions for Dowsing Rod (EMF Reader)

Cut off the bottom wire of the coat hanger

Bend one end of this straight wire to a 45-degree angle

Cut 3 inches from the plastic straw

Place this piece of the plastic straw on the bend end of the wire

Hold this between your thumb and forefinger.

Be sure to hold this away from your face and watch it sway back and forth or spin around. This swaying or spinning is your energy level.

Directions for Using:

Show the tool to your pet. Give it time to sniff it. Lay it on the pet's back. It needs to learn that it is not a danger.
If you choose to use your hands, place your hands or four fingers on each hand about 2 inches above the chakra for small animals and 2 to 4 inches for larger animals. This may vary due to your vibrational sensitivity.

If you feel a small or slight vibration or a subtle warmth that indicates no blockage. If, on the other hand, you feel nothing this can be an indication of a blockage. Take a minute and gently rub your hands together.

Then either lay your hands on the chakra or keep them just above the chakra. Keep your hands in that position for several minutes. Repeat in 2 hours.

If you do not notice a positive change, call your veterinarian.

CHAPTER THREE

CHAKRA TUNING

Each chakra has a specific vibration The following chart shows the Hertz for each of the traditional chakras.

Chakra and Hertz Chart

Chakra	Hertz
Root	396
Sacral	417
Solar Plexus	528
Third Eye	852
Throat	741
Heart	639
Crown	963

Using vocal sounds allows you to break the blockage that may be causing your pet discomfort. Holding the vocal sound may take some practice. The following chart includes the hertz and the vocal sound to use with each chakra.

CHAKRA	HERTZ	VOCAL SOUND
Root	256	Uh
Sacral	288	Ooh
Solar Plexus	320	Oh
Heart	341	Ah
Throat	384	Eye
Brow	448	Aye

If you do not wish to vocalize, consider using a recording of the Solfeggio Sound. Solfeggio frequencies are a set of ancient tones that have a number of healing benefits for humans, animals, and plants. The following chart provides the Solfeggio Hertz for each of the eight animal Chakras.

CHAKRA   **SOLFEGGIO HERTZ**
Root   396Hz
Sacral   417Hz
Solar Plexus   528Hz
Heart   639Hz
Throat   741Hz
Brow   852Hz
Crown   963Hz
Brachial   10KHz*

*CAUTION: The suggested hertz for the Brachial Chakra is a very high frequency and care should be taken before applying it directly to a dog or cat. If you decide to try it, do so at a very low volume. Serious hearing loss could result.

ACTIVITY 2
Boom, Boom It

<u>What You Will Need:</u>
> A mini ultra slim Bluetooth speaker that works with an iPhone, iPad, laptop.
> A recording of Solfeggio sounds.

<u>Directions:</u>
Introduce the mini speaker to your pet. Once your pet is comfortable with the setting, place the speaker near the cat or dog's blocked chakra. Underneath the pet's bed or pillow.

Play the Solfeggio for 10 minutes, twice a day for 5 days. Do not play it loud but softly. Animal ears are very sensitive. Your pet may reject the sound. If it does not, and if there is no improvement contact your veterinarian.

If your pet is small enough to sit in your lap and if you have room for the mini speaker, try using it that way.

BHRAMARI PRANAYAMA (HUMMING)

The term Bhramari is a Sanskrit word which means bee. Pranayama means 'breath of life.' In the Bhramari Pranayama breathing technique the humming sound resembling that of bee, that is, one produces a low-pitched humming audible sound. One does this as long as possible, during the exhalation of breath.

What has this got to do with healing an animal's blocked chakra? Studies show that pets can react and do react to different types of sounds. Dogs and cats respond differently to sounds and that response is based on their preference for certain tempo and volume, for example, in calming. Humming is an easy and natural human experience and it can bring about positive change. For your pets, humming helps increase Nitric Oxide, stimulates their vagus nerve (dogs have two), and improves heart rate variability. Added to this, is the improvement in your pet's chakra functions.

ACTIVITY 3
DOING THE HUM

<u>Directions:</u>

After determining which chakra needs 'fixing,' place your dominate hand on that chakra and then begin to hum the word hum. Inhale through your nose, with your mouth closed. Exhale through your nose while making a hummmmm sound. Feel the vibration around your lips. Do this until the sound naturally stops.

Do this five to ten minute, depending on your pet's cooperation. Apply this to your pet twice a week.

By the way, Jonathon Goldman and Andi Goldman's book, *The Humming Effect: Sound Healing for Health and Happiness (Hay House, 2017)* is an excellent resource for humming.

CHAPTER FOUR

CRYSTALS

Another way to help the healing processes of the animals' chakras is to add crystals to the treatment regimen. Shaman didn't use the word crystal. They called them "stones." Each of the major chakras may have more than one associated crystal. The following chart suggests a crystal for each chakra

Chakra	**Crystal**
Root	Brick Red Jasper
Sacral	Red Carnelian
Solar Plexus	Yellow Aventurine
Heart	Green Aventurine
Throat	Lapis Lazuli
Brow	Blue Aventurine
Crown	Amethyst
Brachial	Tiger's Eye

Because each of the suggested crystals have more than one qualifying attribute that is chakra appropriate, we provide a brief discussion of each.

The word *jasper* is derived from the Greek *iaspi* which means "spotted stone." Jasper is classified as an opaque chalcedony which is a general term used for all varieties of quartz. They come in a variety of colors. Brick Red Jasper is almost one pure color; whereas, other Jaspers will have other colors mixed in. Long a favorite among the ancient cultures, it holds a high regard in today's world as a powerful healing stone and offers strong protection. It helps balance dynamic energy; thus, relieving stress.

Like Jasper, Red Carnelian is a member of the Chalcedony grouping and comes in reddish brown colors. Known as the Sunset Stone, it builds power and self-confidence. It cleanses negativity, and sense of failure.

Yellow Aventurine is part of the quartz family of crystals. It is the crystal to unblock issues in the Solar Plexus and allow optimal growth— physical and emotional.

Green Aventurine, like its cousin Yellow Aventurine, Is part of the quartz family of crystals. Known as "the Stone of Opportunity," it is a wonderful healing stone and especially for cleansing your pet's vital organs. Additionally, Green Aventurine is an excellent crystal for dissolving negative behavior and neutralizing EMF in your pet's sleeping area.

Lapis Lazuli is a mixture of Lazurite, Calcite, Pyrite, and Sodalite. Its name, like its composition contains more than just one word. Lapis, from the Latin, means stone, and lāzaward from the Persian meaning sky. It embodies inner vision, and self-confidence.

According to some authorities, **Blue Aventurine** is one of the rarest aventurine stones. It comes in many shades and is an excellent stone for heart health by establishing a sense of inner tranquility.

Amethyst has been held in high esteem for over two thousand years for spiritual and healing qualities. It helps reduce tension, promotes a state of calmness and well-being.

Tigers Eye is a member of the Chalcedony family. It is reddish brown with iron stripes. It is a wonderful stone to use for balance and well-being. It is especially helpful in bringing about balance in the endocrine system.

It is natural to want to know what areas specific steps, elixirs, and crystal help heal. The following chart, *Crystal, and Their Healing Properties*, provides a quick summary of what issue each of the suggested crystals help.

CRYSTALS AND THEIR HEALING PROPERTIES

Crystal	Healing Property
Brick Red Jasper	Relieves stress
Red Carnelian	Relieves Negativity
Yellow Aventurine	Optimizes growth
Green Aventurine	Emotional Issues
Lapis Lazul	Confidence
Blue Aventurine	Tranquility
Amethyst	Protection
Tiger's Eye	Confidence

ACTIVITY 4
Bag It

Depending of the chakra that has a blockage, select the appropriate crystal, and place several small pieces or one large piece in a cloth bag, tie it tightly and place it under the pet's bed.

Depending on your animal, make sure the bag is securely fastened to the pet's bed.

Leave the bag of crystals in place for one week.

ACTIVITY 5
Chain It

Once you have determined the Chakra with an issue, select the appropriate crystal. You should have at least three pieces.

Wrap each piece in a jeweler's wire. Attach these to a small chain. Make sure they are secure. Fasten the chain to the dog's collar or cat's flea color.

ACTIVITY 6
Water, Water

Be sure that the crystals you have selected are non-soluble. Depending of the size of the crystals, place 2 to 3 in a quart of distilled water. Use a quart jar with a lid. Place in your refrigerator for 24 hours. Remove the crystals, sanitize them, and recharge them for use. Give 1/4 cup to your pet to drink once a day until the crystal infused water is depleted. Repeat if necessary.

As various other things in our lives are, crystals also have to be cleaned. Like humans and animals, crystals carry germs. There are other reasons for cleansing crystals. Crystals absorb energy; both positive and negative energy. If you buy your crystals in a shop or have them shipped to you any number of people could have handled them and could have left germs as well as negative energy.

Once negative energy sets in, it will continue to attract and build more negativity. This negativity comes from the crystal's surroundings, EMF, and from its use with clients who are negative. This makes any use of the crystal in healing ineffective.

Cleansing your crystals will increase their usefulness and enhance their healing powers. It will also increase their lifespan, and effectiveness. Here are some ways to cleanse your crystals. But first a WARNING!

 Be sure your crystals can be placed in water. DO NOT use water to cleanse Selenite or Desert Rose. They will dissolve! The following crystals will crumble when exposed to water: Sulfur, Kyanite, Zeolite, and Azurite.

If you are making crystal elixirs or skincare lotions it has been suggested by some specialists that you wash those crystals with mild soap and water. Experience has suggested a problem with left-over soap on the crystal. I prefer using lavender hydrosol. Spray the crystals with the hydrosol and then rinse with water. The Lavender Hydrosol is an excellent disinfectant and will not create issue for making crystal elixirs or skincare lotions.

In addition to using water and soap to cleanse crystals there are six other regularly suggested ways or methods for cleansing your crystals.

1.Salt Water: Soak the crystals in a very mild sea salt water -; rinse with clear water, pat dry with a soft cloth. Do not use with crystals that do not tolerate water. Additionally, do not use with Pyrite, Lapis Lazuli, Opal, or Hematite.

2. Rice: Brown rice is often suggested. White rice also works. Use a clean saucer or other small glass dish. Place enough rice in the dish to just cover the bottom. Add the crystal(s). Be sure to place the dish away from electronic devices and or direct sunlight. Wait 24 hours, remove the crystal(s) and rinse.

3, Fire: Light a wax candle. Pass a crystal through the flame, being careful not to burn yourself. Repeat several times or as often as necessary until you feel the crystal is clean. This is my least favorite.

4 Sunlight: Place a crystal or several on a clean paper plate. Set this in direct sunlight for two to three hours. You have to determine the time. Some crystals, Amethyst for example, may fade and become less effective.

5.Moonlight: Place crystals on a paper plate and set this in a safe location where it will be in the moonlight most of the night. Remember nocturnal animals may be attracted to a shiny object.

6, Smudging: Long a favorite among healers, burning a sage stick is an easy way to eliminate negative energy from your crystal. Palo Santo and Cedar also work well for smudging.

Just as your laptop, iPad, cellphone and other electronic devices, crystals also, have to be recharged. It is generally accepted that crystals have their own energy field and with continual use that field is reduced and becomes ineffective. It they are not cleansed of dust, grime from handling, and EMF pollution, crystals expel negativity.

In addition to replenishing energy, charging often enhances current energy levels of crystals. Like cleansing, there are several ways to charge your crystals. These charging methods range from water treatment, placing crystals in sea salt, burying them in the ground to giving them Reiki treatment. Several of the cleansing methods can be used to charge crystals.

CHAPTER FIVE

ANIMAL CHAKRAS AND ESSENTIAL OILS

Admittedly, there is controversy over the use of essential oils and its use in the treatment of animals. But first, what is an essential oil? An essential oil is a concentrated hydrophobic liquid and is often called volatile or ethereal oils. By whatever name

they are called, they are made from plants. There are nine methods used for creating an essential oil: Steam Distillation, Absolutes, Mechanical, CO_2, Cold Press, Water Distillation, Solvent Extraction, Enfleurage, and Maceration. By far the most popular method of creating an essential oil is Steam Distillation as it is for me.

Any more than you should do to yourself, do not apply essential oils directly to the skin of your pets. And only when they are mixed with a carrier oil and under the supervision of a veterinarian. Those essential oils that are deemed safe to use with pets include the following and the chakra to which they may be used:

ESSENTIAL OIL AND CHAKRAS

OILS	**CHAKRAS**
Cedarwood	Root
Turmeric	Sacral
Lemon	Solar Plexus
Copaiba	Heart
Arborvitae	Throat
Petitgrain	Brow
Frankincense	Crown
Lavender	Brachial

Several aspects of essential oils that may have a direct impact on your pets. First, they may help create a sense of inner peace for the pet. Second, because of the calming effect, your pet may show an improved self-esteem. This is particularly true of rescued pets. Depending on the essential oil being used, the pet's temperament be improved, and finally, the chosen oil may help a pet's wound to heal.

Unfortunately, there is a negative side to the use of essential oils and this applies to pets as well as to humans. Generally, those oils that are highly fragrant are the culprits. They contain the following irritants: limonene, citronellol, eugenol, and linalool. If you use an essential oil of high fragrance, it is a good idea to test it with your pet before using it. Activity 7 provides testing instructions.

The following chart shows essential oils that should never be used on cats and the problems they create.

TEN ESSENTAIL OILS THAT SHOULD NEVER BE USED ON CATS

The Essential Oil	What it causes
Basil	Liver Disease
Bergamot	Liver Disease
Cinnamon	Diarrhea
Clove	Respiratory
Fennel	Diarrhea
Marijuana	Seizures
Oregano	Liver Disease
Peppermint	Dehydration
Tea Tree	Paralysis
Thyme	Respiratory

According to the ASPCA and the CMVA the following essential oils are listed as toxic: Clary Sage, Eucalyptus, European Pennyroyal, Geranium, Sandalwood, Wormseed, and Ylang-Ylang.

ACTIVITY 7

What You Will Need:
The oil of choice for testing
1-inch piece of cotton cloth or three cotton balls.
An eye dropper
Carrier oil such as jojoba

Directions:
Mix 5 drops of the essential oil with 15 drops of the carrier oil
Soak the cloth or cotton balls with the oil
Place under the pet's bed or blanket

Leave it for 3 days. Discard

***

Check regularly each day to make sure your cat is not experiencing any negative reaction. If any signs appear, immediately stop using the treatment, clean the cat's bed, and contact your veterinarian.

Finally, if you have concerns about that degree of exposure to an essential oil, placing 2 or 3 drops in a diffuser is an acceptable substitute. Place the diffuser in the room where the cat beds down for the night. Set the timer for nor more than one hour.

If you pet shows no negative signs in the morning, continue with the diffuser for two or three days.

Remember, these activities presented here are not substitutes for medical treatment and are offered only as suggested supportive treatment.

CHAPTER SIX

LEARNING TO SEE AURAS

An aura has been defined as reflected energy surrounding animals, humans, and plants. Auras are not static. Auras evolve with the living entity. An aura is sometimes called Human Energy Field or HEF.

A clear and precise history of the origin of the aura concept is difficult to pinpoint. However, one source suggests early Egyptians advanced the notion of a personal essence (energy) called the *Ka*. Ancient Greek philosophers, Aristotle and Plato discussed a halo that appeared around certain individuals. They used the word *aureole* from which we get the word aura. Early Chinese medicine referred to Qi, pronounced as chi. In Indian Hinduism this energy is called prana while in Buddhism it is *nmitta*.

Jumping to the 19th century, it has been suggested that the concept of aura came about from the works of Charles Webster Leadbeater (1854-1934) and psychic healer, Edgar Cayce (1877-1945).

Cayce's statement is of interest: "An aura is an effect, not a cause" still holds sway today. In the same twenty-page essay, Cayce continues: "Every atom, every molecule, every group of atoms and molecules, however, simple, or complex, however large, or small, tells the story of itself, its pattern, its purpose, through the vibrations which emanate from it. Colors are the perceptions of these vibrations by the human eye." (Auras: An Essay on the Meaning of Colors. Edgar Cayce. Reprint Edition. A.R.E. Press. 1973. Virginia Beach, Virginia.)

The aura is connected to the energy centers of your pet's body. These chakras are composed of 8 layers which in turn, radiate in colors. Colors are not just suggestive of blockages or other issues. They suggest wellness and strength.

And it is to that end, that the material contained herein is dedicated to making you a healing companion for your pet.

For many of you, it may seem to be an impossible task to even see your pet's aura let alone read what it means. It takes some practice to see auras whether it's your pet, a tree, a flower, or family member.

First, and foremost, your eye muscles have to be trained. The following exercises are to help train your eye as well as your sensitivity. One of the first things I was taught when I was learning to read auras was to accept the fact that not everyone sees the same thing and second, to be physically more sensitive.

Activity 8, **Feeling the Force** is designed to help you be more sensitive to subtle energy fluctuations.

It helps you feel energy. Instead of reminding you that practice makes perfect I prefer to say *practice makes potentiality possible.*

ACTIVITY 8
Feeling the Force

<u>Directions:</u>

Wash your hands with mild soap and in temped water.

Using a soft towel, pat dry your hands.

Shake both hands for about 90 seconds.

Place the palms of your hands facing each other and vigorously rub them together.

Now place both hands about a quarter inch above your forehead.

You should feel a slight pressure and even warmth. That is your aura.

A variation on this exercise is to have a family member or a friend rub their hands and then bring your hands close to their hands.

One of the issues you may experience as you train your eyes may be a challenge. That issue is overly focusing or putting it another way, "trying too hard." If you feel that is an issue Activity 9, **Feeling Fine**, will help you get through that. For this activity, you will need a family member or a friend to help you.

ACIVITY 9
Feeling Fine

What You Need:

A comfortable chair (Not one to nap in) and a relative or a friend

Directions:

Sit in the chair. Close your eyes and take 5 deep breaths. Have your relative or friend stand 4 feet away from you.

Next, have your friend slowly move to 3 feet of you, with extended arms and hands pointing at you and but touching you. (A distance adjustment may have to be made depending on the length of the person's arms and hands. They should be 2 feet from you.)

At the point you feel or sense them, tell your relative or friend. Open your eyes.

You have felt the Etheric Field. Note how close they were to you.

Do this every other day for two weeks. It will help you, if you establish a specific time of day.

Activity 10 is one of my favorites only because I do it after I have gone to bed. Being in bed, however, is not a requirement for this activity. Additionally, there are a couple of variations that will help strengthen you power of observation.

ACTIVITY TEN
Two Fingers; Then Five

To begin, blink your eyes 5 times. Not fast; just normal then take 5 deep breaths. Look up without turning your head upward. Look down without lowering your head. The reason for doing is to defocus your eyes.

Now take the index finger of each hand and bring them together end to end.

Concentrate on the area around your two touching fingers. This may take some time. Patience is the operative word.

Look at the area around your two fingers. Look for a faint glow surrounding these two fingers. It may appear to be rising from the two fingers. Here's a hint: It works better when holding your fingers 8 to 10 inches from your nose and if you hold your fingers against a plain background. The bedroom ceiling is a good choice.

One more practice activity.

ACTIVITY 11
The Eyes Have It

You will need a relative or a friend, a light-colored wall, and defused lighting. In addition to being a light color, a pale white or light beige, the wall should be fee of pictures, photos, or other decorations.

Have your relative or friend sit in front of the wall; either in a chair or on the floor. Do not have a light shining directly on them.

Sit in a chair or on the floor facing relative or friend. About four to five feet away will work.

Take 5 deep breaths, rotate your shoulders. The point is to relax.

Look at your relative or friend's head. Focus your attention in the center of their forehead.

You should feel and sense your eyes going out of focus. Good.

You should begin to see a radiance around your relative or friend's head. It might be faint yellow-white glow. There might be some very slow movement in the radiance.

This is the aura. It may change in colors and size.

ACTIVITY 12
Plant It

House plants are an excellent source of practice material. House plants are generally not huge. Fortunately, size is not a requirement.

Select a plant, place it so it is 1 to 2 feet from a plain wall. The plant should not be in bright light.

Squint your eyes and look at the plant.

Notice the slight shimmer along the plant's leaves. Check the color. The color and intensity of the aura will tell you if the plant is well or suffering an illness.

CHAPTER SEVEN

AURA CHECK-UP FOR YOUR PET

Treating an ill pet from ancient traditions such as Chakras, Auras, Reiki, or Shamanism can and often does vary. This variance depends on one's religious, cultural beliefs, and practices.

Applying any of the techniques, methods, or suggestions presented throughout this book may be effective and other times they may not. In reality, this isn't any different than modern medical practices. A contemporary medical practitioner may provide a treatment and it doesn't resolve the issue. Something else is then tried. Some things may work with your pet and others may not. It is for that reasons that several activities are included.

The color, brightness, and strength of the aura surrounding your pet reflects its physical and emotional condition, personality, and overall behavior.

If any of the basic auric colors are pale or faded, it is suggestive that your pet is not up to par. If, for example, yellow is very pale, it is indicative that your pet is ill. If the aura you see is black your pet is definitely ill and you should begin treatment and contact your pet 's doctor.

Performing an aura check on your pet falls into the category of potentialities and not always realities. Practice reduces the opportunity of misreading your pet's aura.

One way to build confidence and effectiveness in aura reading is practice. Practice is and has been the major operative word throughout this course.

Recognizing your time is valuable and to save you time the aura colors and their implied meanings are again listed. First listed are the chakras for cats; second will be for dogs.

CAT AURAS AND THEIR MEANINGS

COLOR	MEANING
Red	Energetic
Orange	Social
Yellow	Happy
Green	Healthy
Blue	Calm
Purple	Empathy
Black	Ill
White	Positive

DOG AURAS AND THEIR MEANINGS

COLOR	MEANING
Red	Energetic
Orange	Playful
Yellow	Curious
Green	Calm
Blue	Sensitive
Purple	Empathy
Black	Ill
White	Peaceful

The colors and their suggested meanings are subjective and are not scientifically based. Here is an example: An auric reader reports a dull and dirty red aura surrounding your cat. The interpretation goes something like this: Your cat is angry, fearful, unstable, weak, suffering a trauma, and seeks revenge. A second reader might say the dull and dirty red aura means your cat is bored. Which is correct? Which should you believe?

The main reason for learning to read your pet's aura is to eliminate off the cuff subjective aura readings. Your reading will be subjective, but when you do several readings over time, those readings will be consistent and consequently more reliable.

You will need to build your pet's acceptance and your security in aura reading. The old saying, "Practice makes perfect" holds true when it comes to aura diagnosis.

There is only one activity for this short module. Its purpose is to provide:

Practice in seeing your pet's aura, and to

Look for subtle changes in the aura colors

Note any changes in the dominate color(s)

Note any changes in the width of the color strips

Keeping regular notes to compare your aura readings

ACTIVITY 13
Write It Up

What You Will Need:

A note pad with pen or pencil

If you prefer, you may use a tape recorder, cell phone, or iPad.

A reasonably blank wall at your pet's level. If that is not easily available consider a large trifold foam presentation board or it may be made of cardboard. It should be large enough for you pet to sit in front of it.

Of course, your pet.

Directions:

If you have more than one pet, do one at a time and keep them separated during the aura scan.

Let your pet sniff your notepad and whatever else you will be using to take notes

You may need to lay down with your pet either in front of the wall or presentation board. Do this a couple times a day for a couple of days. The purpose here is to make your pet feel comfortable and not engage in exploring.

Teach your pet to stay in place for a few minutes. Maybe 3 minutes. Just long enough for you to get a good look.

Sit in front of your pet and look at it. Focus about 2 inches above its body.

Make notes on what you saw. Now if you didn't see anything, that's okay. Remember, practice.

Do this at the same time every day for 5 days. Unless you detect something negative, wait a full seek before doing another reading. Follow the same procedure as for the first week. Keep notes.

If there has been an issue detected, do a healing on your pet. If you see no improvement, contact your veterinarian.

A final reminder of the four most common indicators that your pet is experiencing a Chakra blockage or an imbalance:

Behavioral changes such as bouts of aggression, anxiety, or withdrawal

Physical issues such as being touchy, frequent licking of a chakra area

Change in appetite

Excessive meowing or whining

Sudden loss of energy

Excessive sleeping.

Constant licking of paws

CHAPTER EIGHT

KIRLIAN PHOTOGRAPHY AND YOUR PET

Simply put, Kirlian photography is a technique for recording photographic images of *corona discharges.*

A *corona discharge* is an electrical discharge caused by the ionization of a fluid such as air surrounding a conductor carrying a high voltage. The result is aura photographs.

The early development of this type of photography began In 1939 with electrical engineer Semyon Kirlian and his wife, Valentina. This Russian couple had observed a hospital patient who was receiving medical treatment involving a high-frequency generator. What they witnessed was a glow around the patient's skin—an aura of light.

Nearly twenty years later, the Kilian's reported the results of their studies. Unfortunately, their work remained nearly unknown until 1970. At that time, two Americans, Lynn Schroeder, and Sheila Ostrander, published a book, *Psychic Discoveries Behind the Iron Curtain*. (*Ostrander, S.; Schroeder, L. (1970). Psi Discoveries Behind the Iron Curtain. Prentice-Hall.*)

Fortunately, Kirlian photography does not require the use of a camera or a lens because it is a contact print process. Cameras are expensive; some have a $10,000 price tag.

It is possible to use a transparent electrode in place of the high-voltage discharge plate, for capturing the resulting corona discharge with a standard photo or video camera.

The advantages offered by Kirlian photography for healing practitioners is the visualization it offers as a diagnostic tool. It adds one more level for diagnosing. It is not a replacement.

Despite the praise and anecdotal reporting, there is very little scientific research in the use of or the impact of Kirlian Photography on animals it still holds value. First, it has value as a potential diagnostic tool for your pet. Second, it allows you to monitor the animals' Chakras; for instance, is there a change in colors or aura patterns? Third, there is the potential integration with holistic care that involves standard medical practices.

An expensive camera is not a prerequisite of Kirlian Photography. In fact, a camera is not required. To capture the coronal discharges which gives you the aura the following material is needed: high voltage power supply, metal plate, photographic plate, and a darkroom.

Did you notice anything in the above requirements that might suggest this is something you should not even attempt with your pet? High voltage!

This approach is fine for plant parts, but not for animals. Your pet would have to be placed on the metal plate that is connected to the high voltage.

I have included this very brief discussion to forewarn you. Go to a professional who has cameras.

There are studios that offer Kirlian Photography, sometimes called aura photography. The issue for the pet owner is to make sure their pet remains perfectly still for 10 to 15 seconds. Owners can't sit with the pet or hold it. Their energy interferes with the pet's.

By-the-way, there is GDV Camera Systems available. It was developed by Konstantin Korotkov. The Gas Discharge Visualization Camera System allows a recording of the process and the interpretation of the images with a computer.

CHAPTER NINE

FOOD FOR THE CHAKRAS

Pet foods are in major competition and controversy over safety, health promotion, dry vs wet food, and refrigerated as opposed to canned. To give you some idea as to the importance of pet foods, $64.4 billion dollars was spent on pet food in 2023 in the United States. $133.9 billion was spent worldwide. The United States' Federal Food, Drug, and Cosmetic Act requires all animal foods to be safe to eat, produced under sanitary conditions, contain no harmful substances, and to be truthfully labeled.

Concerns about "grain free" and non-grain-free foods is legitimate. It has been found that some "grain-free" pet foods contained high amounts of peas, lentils, legumes, potatoes. Pet foods should be high in nutrients that help healing, vibrational levels, and balanced chakras.

The following suggestions for each of the 8 chakras are just that—suggestions. Check the pet food you buy for the ingredients. If you can't find canned or packaged animal food containing these suggested additional foods, you may have to go to a place that custom makes pet foods. You may have to make some adjustments to the kind and amount you provide for your pet. Always check with your veterinarian before embarking upon a completely new food regimen.

Research has demonstrated disagreement over what foods animals may or may not eat. And that holds true to the suggested foods listed here. A recent example illustrates the issue: One source suggest feeding dark chocolate to cats and dogs. Other sources adamantly say do not feed chocolate to cats and dogs.

Root Chakra is the energy center and because it supports the entire system of your pet, it is also the one that generally experiences blockages. The foods you want to consider are those that are rich in protein and are grounding for your pet. Among these are: Lean meats such as chicken, turkey. Vegetables such as carrots and sweet potatoes and pumpkin. These foods are helpful if your pet is suffering from anxiety.

Sacral Chakra, the reproductive center, can be brought into balance by adding Omega-3 fatty acids contained in fish, especially salmon and tuna. Eggs are an excellent source for choline, a strong support of neurological functions. Two fruits, oranges, and mangoes, high in antioxidants, promotes vitality.

Solar Plexus requires foods that promotes metabolism and digestion. Suggested foods included brown rice and oats for energy and gut health. Yellow Squash and yellow peppers are vitamin rich and help digestion. Another fruit is pineapple. It helps reduce inflammation.

Heart Chakra is more than just a pump that holds the life line, but messages the body with love and affection. Spinach and Kayle support the cardiovascular system. Green beans boosts heart health. Apples, high in antioxidants enhances the respiratory system.

Throat Chakra is the major communication devise. Blueberries help to promote communication. Honey enhances vocal clarity. Chamomile Tea calms the nerves and supports communication.

Third Eye Chakra requires foods that support mental functions. Suggested foods include purple grapes and walnuts.

Crown Chakra benefits from coconut oil, lavender tea, and amaranth which supports overall health.

Brachial Chakra, the main energy center of animals is supported and enhanced by carrots, sweet potatoes, mangos, and peaches.

SELECTING FOOD FOR YOUR PET

Pet food ads are more than abundant in today's television world. They are so extensive, competitive, and confusing that you often don't know what food to offer to your pet. What then can you do?

You can check with your pet's veterinarian to see if your pet has any dietary anomalies and go from there in deciding on foods. Some veterinarians sell pet foods.

And there are companies that produce specialized pet foods. Inven.ai (https://www.Inven.ai) lists 21 pet food companies that produce specialized pet foods. Here are a few of those listed companies:

Hill's Pet Nutrition (hillspet.com) Located in the United States

Blue Buffalo (bluefuffalo.com) Located in the United States,

Royal Canin (roualcanin.com) Located in France,

Special Dog Company (specialdog.com.br) Located in Brazil, and

Inspired Pet Nutrition (ipn.co.uk) Located in England, and

Petcurean (petcurean.com) Located in Canada.

SELECTING COMMERICAL CAT AND DOG FOOD

Things You Want in a Pet Food:

Make sure the first listed ingredient is an " animal-based" protein

Check that the preservatives are natural; vitamin C, and E

Check that essential fatty acids are in the food

Things You Want to Avoid in Pet Food

Wheat middling's and corn gluten

Avoid foods containing Ethoxyquin and propylene glycol

Avoid phosphoric acid and other flavor enhancers, and

Azo, Azo dyes and sodium nitrite and other artificial colors.

DO IT YOURSELF

For those who like to prepare their own pet foods and have the time to do so, two recipes are suggested.

<u>Protein, If you Please</u>
You will need the following ingredients:
1 chicken breast, deboned
1 chicken liver
1 can of non-oil-based sardines
1 cup of chopped broccoli Add one chopped carrot
Two tablespoons of olive oil

<u>Directions:</u>
Cook the chicken breast (your choice of procedure, i.e. roast, pan fry, instant pot, grill) Don't overcook.

Cut the chicken into small chunks

Drain the can of sardines

Cook the broccoli and carrot

Use a food processor to grind up the ingredients.

Give 4 ounces to your cat or dog. Size of your pet may dictate the amount of the serving.

Package the left-over food and freeze for another day.

Cooking It Slow

You will need the following ingredients:
4 cups of low sodium chicken broth,
1 cup of water,
1 can of pumpkin
2 cans of French Green Beans
I cup of cooked brown rice
3 cans of sardines packed*
2 to 3 cups of fresh spinach, chopped loosely
2 large eggs
1 pkg of chicken breasts

Add all the ingredients with the exceptions of the chicken and sardines to a large pot. Turn heat to low. Thoroughly stir the ingredients.

Add the chicken. Make sure there is enough liquid to completely cover the chicken. Cook until the chicken is done. Remove the chicken and let it cool.

Shred the chicken until it is fine. Add it back to the pot along with the sardines. Stir until all ingredients are thoroughly mixed.

Once cool, add one cup of the mixture to a freezer bag. Do this until all the mixture has been bagged. Freeze. When needed, remove a bag, let it thaw in the refrigerator. Give 2 to 3 tbsp as a serving to your cat each day along with its regular food.

CHAPTER TEN

REIKI FOR THE CHAKRAS

Briefly, what is Reiki. The word from the Japanese, means "Life Force" or "Energy." Reiki practitioners believe that all things vibrate and thusly, create energy. Energy flows through a Reiki Practitioner to a client. Here's the catch: It is not just the practitioner's energy, it's the energy of the universe. The practitioner is a conduit.

The National Center for Complementary and Integrative Health has stated, "Reiki is a complimentary medicine practice that uses putative energy fields to affect health."

Sometime in 1994 the National Institute of Health came up with the term *Biofield* to describe the energy and information surrounding and interpenetrating the human body as well as animals.

This Biofield is composed of measurable electromagnetic energy. Within this is a subtle energy called *Chi.* In this book, it has been called aura.

Generally, a Reiki Practitioner does not place her/his hands directly on a client. They allow their hands to float about an inch to two inches above the client. This is especially true for the treatment of animals.

Not all animals like to be touched; humans are not any different. However, there are some Reiki Practitioners who are touchers as is the author of this book. What then, do I recommend if you are dealing with a cat or dog that doesn't like a stranger touching them?

Warn the practitioner that your pet doesn't appreciate strangers touching them.

Shake hands with the Reiki healer and let your pet sniff your hand.

Then have your Reiki healer extend one hand toward your pet. Don't attempt a forced sniff. Wait. Then try it again. If the pet sniffs the Practitioner's hand, have that person, extend his/her hand to the pet's head. Repeat this a couple more times. If the pet is favorably responsive, then continue with the exam and treatment. The pets' reaction will vary. As it will after treatment has been completed.

A recent experience will illustrate. A German Shepherd was ill and was scheduled to be put-down. Its owners were heartbroken. The dog was specifically trained as a service dog for a person with MS. During the Reiki session, the dog placed it large paw on my hand, lifted its head and kissed me. The owners were totally blown away. The dog had never responded to anyone with such affection including them.

Reiki Practitioners use a variety of symbols during a healing session. Each symbol represents a different characteristic of Reiki energy.

Back in the day, the Reiki symbols were highly guarded secrets. Today, one can find them on the Internet. Two of the first symbols one learns in Reiki training and also the most important and powerful are Cho-ko-rei (Pronounced Koo Ko Ray) and Sei He-Ki(Pronounced Say Hi Key).

Cho-ko-rei literally means place all the powers of the universe here. It also immediately increases the practitioner's ability to channel universal energies.

The standard international physical representation of this symbol is shown here.

As you say this symbol three times, draw It with your finger in the palm of your dominate hand.
Next, draw the second symbol in your dominate hand and say its name three times as you do so.

SEI HE KI

Sei-He-Ki brings the mind and body together to focus and harmonize the subconsciousness with the physical body; thus, allowing healing to occur.

APPLICATION

Here is how you can apply this to your pet if you feel comfortable in doing so.

Once you have said and drawn both symbols in the palm of your dominate hand, rub your hands together for a couple of minutes.

Say the following: "Reiki come near and do whatever is necessary to heal (name of your pet) for its highest good. Thank you, namaste."

Then slowly move both hands up and down the body of your pet, stopping when you feel nothing. Keep your hands there for a full minute and then move on.

An alternative to drawing these symbols is to create a physical copy of each and look at each as you say the name. Or place the physical copies near your pet and followi the previous procedure.

REFERENCES

Budd, Diane. Energy Medicine for Animals: The Bioenergetics of Animal Healing. Findhorn Press, 2019

Fulton, Elizabeth, and Kathleen Prasad. *Animal Reiki: Using Energy to Heal the Animals in Your Life*. Ulysses Press, 2006.

Gubbins, Cara Dr. Animal Chakras: How to Balance, heal and Unlock Your Pet's Chakras for more harmony, Health, and Happiness. Kindle. 2022

McKenzie, Lynn. *Chakra Healing for Dogs*. Healing Arts Press, 2019.

Ranquet, Joan. Energy Healing for Animals: A Hands-On Guide. Sounds True Publisher, 2015

From the Internet

https://www.katebackdrop.com/blogs/photography-tutorials/aura-photography

ALSO, BY NORMAN W WILSON

Butterflies and All That Jazz with Drs. James G Massey and James A Powell
Windows and Images: An Introduction to the Humanities with Drs. James G. Massey and James A Powell
The Humanities: Contemporary Images
Shamanism: What It's All About
So, You Think You Want to Be a Buddhist?
Promethean Necessity and Its Implications for Humanity
DUH! The American Disaster
The Sayings of Esaugetuh: The Master of Breath
A Shaman's Journey Revealed Through Poetry with Gavriel Navarro
The Shaman's Quest
The Shaman's Transformation
The Shaman's War
The Shaman's Genesis
The Shaman's Revelations,
The Making of a Shaman
Activating Your Spirit Guides
Healing-The Shaman's Way
How to Make Moral and Ethical Decisions: A Guide
Teas Soups and Salads
Reiki: The Instructor's manual
Shamanic Healing Book One
Shamanic Healing Book II Crystals
Healing-The Shaman's Way: Herbs That Help You Heal Book Three
Healing-The Shaman's Way Using Essential Oils Book Four

Healing-The Shaman's Way Using Vibration to Heal Book Five

COURSES AVAILABLE AT UDEMY.COM

Healing-The Shaman's Way
Healing-The Shaman's Way Using Crystals
Healing-The Shaman's Way Using Herbs
Healing-The Shaman's Way using Essential oils
Healing-The Shaman's Way Using Vibration to Heal
Healing-The Shaman's Way Animal Chakras

WEBSITE
Healingtheshamansway.com

On the website you will find dozens of articles you can read for free, YouTube videos to watch for free, and other information that may be of interest. A place to contact me is provided.

ABOUT THE AUTHOR

Norman W Wilson has two doctorates: one in the Humanities and one in Metaphysical Humanism. Wilson is a Cognitive Behavioral Therapist and a retired college professor. He is a trained Shaman, Reiki Master, and Certified Crystal Practitioner. Additionally, he holds certification in aromatherapy and essential oils, Angel Reiki, and Eye Yoga.

www.ingramcontent.com/pod-product-compliance
Lightning Source LLC
Chambersburg PA
CBHW060428050426
42449CB00009B/2190